Looking at Fish

By Sally Cowan

Fish can be little or big.

But they all have gills and fins.

gills

fins

Fish can be very quick
as they swim and swish.

This fish is a red rock cod.

It can look like rocks.

It can dash up
to get little fish.

Some fish do not look much like fish!

This fish is very long.

See it swish!

Some fish have fangs.

They can nip little fish.

They do not nip kids!

This fish is very big!

It has lots of dots on its back.

This big fish can swish its fins.

But it is not in a rush.

This fish has lots
of long fins.

The fins on its back
can sting.

Kids can get fish as pets.

It is fun looking at a fish as it swims and swishes its fins.

CHECKING FOR MEANING

1. What two things do all fish have? *(Literal)*

2. What can a red rock cod look like? *(Literal)*

3. Why do you think some children keep fish as pets? *(Inferential)*

EXTENDING VOCABULARY

dash	What other word in the book has a similar meaning to *dash*? What do these words mean?
fangs	What are *fangs*? What is another word that has a similar meaning? What is special about fangs? What are words you know to describe fangs? E.g. long, sharp.
back	How many sounds are in this word? If you take away the *b* and put another letter or letters at the start, how many new words can you make?

MOVING BEYOND THE TEXT

1. What are gills for? Do people have gills? What do we have instead of gills?

2. How do fins help fish in the water?

3. The red rock cod looks like rocks. How does this help the cod to stay safe in the water?

4. What type of fish do children have as pets? Why?

SPEED SOUNDS

| sh | ch | th | th | ck | ng |

voiced   unvoiced

PRACTICE WORDS

quick

fish

swish

dash

rock

much

fangs

long

Fish

back

rush

sting